St. Francis Poems

St. Francis Poems

David Craig

WIPF & STOCK · Eugene, Oregon

ST. FRANCIS POEMS

Copyright © 2013 David Craig. All rights reserved. Except for brief quotations in critical publications or reviews, no part of this book may be reproduced in any manner without prior written permission from the publisher. Write: Permissions, Wipf and Stock Publishers, 199 W. 8th Ave., Suite 3, Eugene, OR 97401.

Resource Publications
An Imprint of Wipf and Stock Publishers
199 W. 8th Ave., Suite 3
Eugene, OR 97401
www.wipfandstock.com

ISBN 13: 978-1-62564-061-1
Manufactured in the U.S.A.

All scripture quotations, unless otherwise indicated, are taken from the Holy Bible, New International Version®, NIV®. Copyright ©1973, 1978, 1984 by Biblica, Inc.™ Used by permission of Zondervan. All rights reserved worldwide.

Contents

Preface vii

Poems based on *The Three Companions of St. Francis* 1

I	His birth, vanity, frivolity and prodigality 3
II	How he was imprisoned in Perugia 5
III	How the Lord visited Francis' heart 7
IV	How he began to overcome himself 9
V	How the crucifix spoke to him 10
VI	How he escaped from the persecution 11
VII	The hard work and fatigue involved in restoring the church 13

Poems based on the Stigmata Poems from the *Fioretti* 15

The first consideration of the holy stigmata 17
   (The mountain is offered)
The second consideration of the holy stigmata 20
   (Preparation)
The third consideration of the holy stigmata 22
   (Gifts)

Lyrics based on the *Fioretti* 25

I	In this book are contained certain little flowers 27
II	Of Brother Bernard, first companion of St. Francis 29
III	How St. Francis, on account of an uncharitable thought 32
IV	How the angel of God proposed a question 34
V	How the holy Brother Bernard was sent 36
VI	How St. Francis blessed the holy Brother Bernard 38

VII	How St. Francis passed the Lent on an island	40
VIII	How St. Francis showed to Brother Leo perfect joy	42
IX	How St. Francis taught Brother Leo how to answer him	44
X	How Brother Masseo mockingly said all the world	46
XI	How St. Francis made Brother Masseo turn around	48
XII	How St. Francis imposed on Masseo the office of the door	50
XIII	How St. Francis and Brother Masseo praised poverty	52
XIV	As St. Francis and his brothers were speaking	53
XV	How St. Clare ate with St. Francis	55
XVI	How St. Francis received the counsel of St. Clare	57
XVII	How a little boy brother saw Christ	62
XVIII	Of the marvelous chapter held at St. Mary of the Angels	64
XIX	How the vineyard was despoiled	67
XX	Of a wondrously beautiful vision seen by a young brother	70
XXI	Of the miracle at Gubbio	72
XXII	How St. Francis tamed the wild turtledoves	74
XXIII	How St. Francis freed a brother who was in sin	76
XXIV	How St. Francis converted the Soldan	78
XXV	How St. Francis miraculously healed the leper	80

Other versions from the *Fioretti* 83

VI	Francis blessed the holy Brother Bernard	85
XXIII	How Francis freed a brother who was in sin	86

Notes 87

Preface

As Catholics, we have a rich mine of wisdom and stories. No religious tradition has more. And yet how much time do we spend truly meditating on the lives of our saints, on the oral and written tales which have come down to us? The *Fioretti* and *The Three Companions* are part of this deposit. Both medieval texts relay those early days of St. Francis and of his movement; and unfortunately, because of that fact they are too easily dismissed as quaint or excessively childlike. However, as we know, one cannot be too childlike. These stories are important because they give us something of the spirit of St. Francis. They give us a deeper somatic take on people who have done more, who have done it right.

One can read the texts together: the stories and the poems, though that is not necessary as each poem is self-contained. The epigraphs taken from the originals map each piece, announce the "oral" turns one can occasionally expect.

Poems based on
The Three Companions of Saint Francis

I

His birth, vanity, frivolity and prodigality,
how he became generous and charitable to the poor.

Dignity underfoot, he sang so loudly from stumps,
imaginary instruments, that anyone who passed
just had to watch him dare himself, paint his way
into one spiritual corner after another,
until he had no options but severest truth,
in the boisterous rhymes of the troubadours—
set right, by a grin so local it owns the world.

His father had named him after a country
where they knew their fabric, where they valued
life's buckled and measured step
as well as its print, had insisted on a carafe of friends,
ridiculous neighbors—though Pica
wanted the breath of God: Giovanni!

So Francis learned to trade the prayer
the best cloth was for the smiles of new friends.
After work, his mates rang in the chorus
his money made: a cascade of mirth, grace,
surrounded as they all were,
by the cold stones of the only night.

It was all he could give them.

(Was he vain—or just so caught up in his enthusiasms
that they'd begun to make their own demands?)
He'd sew rags to more expensive stuffs,

St. Francis Poems

embracing, again that widow want,
knowing he could not, needing to tell everyone
that as well. So he became a jongleur,
a determined clown, standing in the breech
between the sorrowful truth of this world
and the fleeting faces of his friends.

Courteous in manner, speech, even beyond
his exaggerated self-conscious parody;
everyone knew he could name his own future.
He loved to pose, but only because it promised
what was, in some real way, already here—

until a customer's smirk razed him, brought him down
to squalor, to a world beyond his making,
to people who had nothing to give but their fleas.
It was that wound again,
what he and his friends felt: an abyss
that could not be filled.

Given this, he wondered, where could he live?

II

How he was imprisoned during Assisi's battle with Perugia and of the two visions he later had, wanting to become a knight.

He camped for his new peers,
as if he were that troubadour Bernart de Ventadorn,
fresh from the castle's bread kilns: dancing, skirt lifted
on cold stones, singing too loudly to birds
out the small window, telling rhymes
of fearful Assisian Knights.

Why *should* he worry? The world was new enough;
every morning everywhere mists came,
only to be burnt away by the sun,
so many new people around by afternoon,
no one could've guessed.

And so when the weight of the hours
began to take the measure of one knight's need,
Francis would not back down. He flanked the man,
feinted, sang in bad langue d'oc *because* he was
a merchant's son: "What do you think will become of me?
Rest assured, I will be worshiped throughout the world."

Eventually released, a dream would finally wake him:
past the castles it offered, the legions of runic, rubied arms—
surpassing even his carefully chosen own,
a walled field of shields bronzing sunlight.

Chivalry so moved in him the next morning
that he gave all his clatter away. Friends laughed,
wondered if his stirruped feet were (ever) on the ground.
But Francis, for his part, he figured, yes, yes,
he could give them this; he could give the answer
before its time, be its fool, its peacock,
anything to help them see.

St. Francis Poems

When asked the reason for his glow, Francis
answered largely, as if he were one:
"I shall become a great prince."
Why else were dreams given, but to make us princes
(and holy fools) before we would become one
(preparing him to turn the world upside down)?

He wondered, to what king?
And how could he be a knight and wear the holy ribbons
of Church too? What of his lady-
who-must-be-in-waiting?

The next morning came, and Francis, sitting on a stump,
rejoiced, kept that marvelous engine,
stabled best he could
in his junket-heart.

Poems based on The Three Companions of Saint Francis

III

How the Lord visited Francis' heart for the first time
filling it with marvelous tenderness that gave him strength
to begin to progress spiritually in looking down on himself
and all vanities, in prayer, almsgiving, and poverty.

A party for the new money, and more,
from the very stems of delight: ladies—
each of his pals, now enjoying what was left
of the tipsy night, some steps in front of him,
their misplaced lives, as ever, just out of reach.

Francis, ever the jester, chose to walk behind,
scepter in his hand, dressed as he was,
in silks and tatters, knowing by now that rags
really were riches, either way: metaphor for the chase,
the shell games of wealth and fame;
for that, or for the more quiet, obvious need.

But how could he get his friends to know
what was real, and missing,
what demanded so much?

They came back to him, their captain in mirth
elsewhere, looking up, seemingly lost
in the glorious conflagration of stars.

Was he mooning over the crimson stomacher?

"Yes, you are right!" he answered.
"And I shall take a wife—more noble, wealthy,
and beautiful than any you have never seen."
But they didn't laugh when he said, "Poverty . . .
the one we all chase without knowing it."

And after that day, he never denied an alms

St. Francis Poems

to anyone who asked in God's only name.
Heaping his absent father's table with begged bread,
Francis piled his want high in joyful exasperation,
(in front of his grieving mother: that the world would,
too soon, begin hammering away
at his white-hot enthusiasms, bend him—
all out of shape).

But Francis was, as ever, elsewhere: pressing his face
between Rome's bars, his last flightless bird,
bag of coins, naming Peter's tomb.

And swapping clothes with a beggar,
he tried on his life. Yes! Yes!
These would help him keep himself in a line,
would help him push the world far away,
with its trumpets, bandied names!
This way he'd never confuse himself again.
He'd wake up next to new brothers: lepers,
dew on his rags, soiled feet.

He sang loudly, played fiddlesticks on the open road,
so that the world would be forced to mark him,
hold him to what mattered.

Once back, he didn't share his secret,
because he was betrothed to a lady, Poverty,
a women hidden in so much beauty
that a look from anyone at all
would have violated their first
intimate steps.

Poems based on The Three Companions of Saint Francis

IV

How he began to overcome himself by his dealing with lepers.

Praying loudly, so that God would mark him
mark the degree of his need,
Francis wrapped each day in the fish paper,
soiled strings of his too-personal heart.

Coercing his distant mouth, he made himself kiss
what was left of the leper's hand, fold it,
cracking, crackling over the scarred coins
he'd managed to lodge there.
And the diseased cloth of lip, hot rasp
of peace—returned, marked Francis' face
with all that was rank and squirming inside.

He joined them, a leper before he became one:
these men marked with strength enough
to bear the inside of the cup;
he kissed what he could find, hold of every hand, face,
pressed each to the clear water of his cheeks.

In earnest repetition, he found what he needed:
the swollen face of God, in every moist, crusted curse,
in the drop of every eye.
And because he finally learned
to fully embrace that gift, he had to endure the next:
departure, toward those more obviously afflicted.

St. Francis Poems

V

How the crucifix spoke to him for the first time and how he henceforth carried the passion of Christ in his heart until death.

The corpus strained—against
him, the rut in the land, the stag's opened throat,
every merchant coin; all years before
his own skin would yaw, open its bitter hosanna.

Outside the Portiuncula, he cried out
because no one ever did, because the world would not.

He would make it his rooftop then,
shout in a loud voice, attempt to wake the forest,
all the unfruitful dead beyond.

He'd sprinkled chaste "Brother Ash" on his food
because we never think to do the same.
And because Mary had to rummage,
he rushed to the ground, ate with the pigs.
If the brothers couldn't see how crucial humility was,
how would anyone else?

He'd stop so often, lost in loud sighs:
his aloneness, their burden; he'd provoke,
disrupt them out of any earned rest, meal.
He'd tell them that when they heard the next sigh,
they should praise God for His great condescension;
that they should pray for Francis continually,
whose need was at least as great as their own.

Poems based on The Three Companions of Saint Francis

VI

How he escaped from the persecution of his father and relatives, living with the priest at the church of San Damiano, throwing the money on the window.

Gauds—sold to Foligno, the family's horse
to help it in its acquisitive heave.
Did things matter more than the time left?
And tossing the world onto the sill, he collapsed
under the weight of the wall.

His father spread out beneath his table.
Was God now asking for ten percent of his son too?
Or had the fool gone off at another deep end?

So Pietro left to find out just how strongly Francis stood.
But when his son hid from the commandments,
he irked: for exactly what life
was this preparing him?

Francis prayed hard that God
who never showed Himself, would—
just this once; days later finding courage
in the only place it is ever offered: in darkness.

If God were with him, after all,
who could stand against?
Many as it turned out. Mud flew in the streets.

And so his father, again, only wanting his son
to be a man, only wanting him to face his life,
whatever his choices, returned.
Finding only quiet, he collared the boy,
tried to force him to stake out this place he had claimed;
his son had to realize what is cost

St. Francis Poems

to live in the town square.

Francis crowed he'd been freed
by (a convenient) God's grace
(if you asked his father);
and stacking all he did not possess:
"Pietro di Bernadone is no longer my Father . . ."

The ancient stone building
collapsed in on itself. How could his favorite son
so un-love him, a father who only asked
that he stand up for himself, not against him
when the time came.

Led away, the old man clutched his son's clothes,
the Bishop covering Francis with the mantle of church,
his father's earnest hands
with eight centuries of dirt.

VII

The hard work and fatigue involved in restoring the church of San Damiano and how he began to overcome himself by going out for alms.

He praised God throughout the piazzas.
What were they all waiting for, a written invitation?
One had been issued centuries ago!
Or would they all wait for death
to rise up and be counted?

Gathering the alms of the night, in heavy stones,
Francis carried his future, his past:
wet blisters, a stinging chorus.

Many saw him as a Pharisee
calling others the same—what was so new in the gospel
that it had to be yelled across the squares?
But others knew better: felt their collusion
in his cracking bones—they who'd hung back
in every meadow, spilling heaven like wine
under stars, on cold earth.

His father and half-brother came, but
like puppets this time: where they lived, in ridiculous words
they could never speak.

One night he skirted his friends' gambling
debt, balked—at his cowardice.
Then he forced himself, rushed to his knees, sharp dice,
begging for the men's (abashed) forgiveness.
And rejecting a saving face, he stayed there
for too long a time, flushing in the stupidity
that was still saving his life.

Poems based on the Stigmata Section of the *Fioretti*

I

The first consideration of the holy stigmata

(The mountain is offered)

In the forty-third year of his Lord, this little man,
bread for the birds, set off,
(like us, but without our sense of direction).
Oblivious, he joined the green-throated chorus,
petal and pistil, him so sunk in his robe
that you had to go through the smiles to find him.

Earth was a place to be swept, cleaned: broom of dirt
on a sea of dirt, dirt on dirt dancing.
He wanted to be a dandelion spore, tiny
piked pinwheel, silk with a snag, under the great wooden
cart-like wheel of the stars.

Orlando de Chiuse, though, needed his heart-rings numbered,
the years having pushed his best years away.
He saw and detested it, this told joke,
this self, house of cards, shill under money's glass.
He knew his road too well:
a topography of Lent, the burden of the strong—
a collection plate feeding too many hands.

"So great is the good I hope for, all pain delights me . . ."
(This was a different time I should tell you.
People listened. And each, in his own hearing,
received the measure of his pain: small, like the wound

St. Francis Poems

at Jesus' side, stretch and serous fluid,
His labored breathing: the catch there in his ribs—steps,
like an uneven playing field, each of your friends,
one by one, leaving; just you in snake-skin boots,
off the Trailways at the edge of this no-town—
the abandoned gas station, ancient, rusty, shell-white pumps,
the hot crackle of tall, dry grass, sting of grasshoppers
as you walk through a field, duffle bag in hand.

And finally, as you expected, the distant
gathering of skyline, dark, across the southern
Colorado plain: the throat of God.)

Orlando wanted out of himself, whatever that was,
away from the easy laughter of friends.
Yes, "most willingly," Francis would speak to him.
"But first honor thy friends who have invited thee to feast."
(All things in time, at time's pace,
so that time and earth might be valued.)

And then the gift—a mountain: shaven heads,
measuring prayer, two of the wiser friars
on the periphery, where the only voice they heard
was God's: in green leaf, the drinking of water
against sunny banks, refracted feet—how it thirsted one,
for the Spirit and for how *he* meant things;
while the soldiers: in issued boots, the company swill
that grumbled long before rations.

Everyone there beginning in that place everyone does,
out of the place he had settled on: the glamourless gospel,
accomplished through repetition, the showing up:
the time beneath time were time noun enough—
grace and movement, and it's the effort that stays,
the long and quiet patience of God.

Eventually, Masseo de Marignano, Angelo Tancredi,
and Leo, the slow, go with him: James, Peter, John;

Poems based on the Stigmata Section of the Fioretti

they watch him ascend, arms outstretched,
prayers lost in the murmuring leaves.
This was just one more place they could not go:
the slow patrol, the troop with too many voices.
Like us, they knew half the way there: the hand
half-outstretched, the smile plainly given.
When he came down, in strength not his own,
the brothers got him an ass: a different one—
an owner with something to say. "Be nothing
less than people—hope of thee."

Sitting at the foot of the mountain,
ridiculous as the pigeons on his head, his legs,
a bird dropping on his robe, Francis smiled,
his back against a tree. "God is pleased," he said,
"because so much joy is shown by our sisters, the birds."
Men rolled to their feet, followed in the morning mist,
quiet as a suburban lawn, all the mowers asleep.

St. Francis Poems

II
_____

The second consideration of the holy stigmata

(Preparation)

Orlando heaped up food to crowd
the hermit's appetite, wine to wet the failing eye.
Having been fathered himself, Francis opened
under that canopy: the singing of rain on leaves,
like his old happiness, back when stars and clouds
were his great company. Among towering beeches,
God's green hands, only death now between them,
the garden stretching skyward: there before the moon
was moon, cooled as it was, in an egress of geese,

he knew what his brothers needed from him:
that he see who he was. So he walked mountain fissures,
for the congealed, us, who for want of praise
find ourselves split, other. Brothers watched him rise,
bring back their sins, chose, not surprisingly,
wider orbits, around him, themselves.

An angel consoled: "The order stays—the order stays;
even the foulest, if he love the brothers,
mercy," a laundry list for the pure of heart.
"Many will be perfect."

So encouraging his want, he fasted on her life—
where the only voice Mary probably heard
was her own, hanging laundry.
Little tramps: the saint running a Chaplinesque Leo
back and forth to mountain shouting,
finally finding a place where no one
could hear him, inspect.

Poems based on the Stigmata Section of the Fioretti

In silence, Francis would be elsewhere:
a healthy fool made to lie down
and lose what he had grown to love: his ridiculous life,
spooned out of his mouth for his kin, lifted up
like the joyful paralytic, through the roof of heaven.

And because Francis was so small, a devil came:
leaved, licking the hunch on its back—
finally humped, hunkering away
like a sputtering machine clamped to its nut,
without savor, sinking deeper into that desperate glee,
where the only thing to enjoy is self
humoring self, audience of one, returns
diminishing. (And decades later, that same limp
shook a friar between his teeth, spat him down,
the brother crying out as he fell, log bridge on his head.

In an instant, Francis placed him—completed
at the bottom. Meanwhile, his brothers, who had heard the voice
and come for the body, were amazed, found it,
singing, a small log still on his head. What could they do?
They sang as well: the chasm, some with clumps of dirt
on their heads, some arm in arm,
each looking foolish enough to stick out.)

Because Francis was no leader they came,
because he never knew what to say. This time
it would be a bird who would remind him
just how much he needed. It would wake him
for matins, singing or beating its wings.
He'd rise, crack his knuckles, or not when his bones
refused the call, the cold giving-way in them,
when he could feel each move toward parchment:
hollow and gaunt, hungry as his feasting self.

It would sit with him, push pebbles,
his fingers around in the dirt.

St. Francis Poems

III

The third consideration of the holy stigmata
(Gifts)

Yellow-faced, sweaty, in the torch descending,
Leo saw it rest on Francis' head, an absent voice
murmuring in the shake and gilt of late summer leaves.
Turning disobedient to go, he heard his rescue.

At forgiveness's still whole feet, he wept.
And Francis, what could he give
beyond a playful tug on that ear, all of his own?
Yes, God *would do* holy things on this mountain;
all the world will wonder. (Leo wondered—
what more could he do?)

Together they opened the wet Bible
under a slate-grey sky, the shake of trees.
Francis knew it was God who rose in the cold stars
every night, the one who still coddled him
in the breath and muzzle of frozen air.
And the repaying? This small, sad life given,
though he knew it couldn't be little enough.

And so, heavy on the spool of his nature, Francis
turned east, like the Soldan, begged for one last grace—
as God had reckoned all his time: one's delight,
the other's joy—to feel the passion bodily,
where it was real, in the fiber of heart muscle,
burning tendons: the road, dolorosa, beneath his feet.

Poems based on the Stigmata Section of the Fioretti

God inflamed him, upward, in the air to meet
the six-winged seraph, a soul to greet his own:
that surest sun, moving steadily—on the cross;
two white wings extended above his head:
the Father, as ever, being glorified; two wings below,
outstretched, to still the world; and the last,
for Francis only—lost in the glorious white
of twiggy witnesses.

He didn't feel the convulsing: his side
searing without blood—entrails in sunlight.

Francis had seen the truth, and had the sense
to just stand there—lighting up the whole
left side of the mountain. Shepherds saw it for an hour,
looked for wise men. Perhaps a king had decreed it day,
a tax on all who resisted? Silk or the mud they were in?
Hostelry windows blinked; yawns in creaking beds,
a maid turning up and out, butter churn in hand,
cold as the months to come; while Romagna muleteers,
believing that the first light was dawn,
saw it cease. When the natural sun rose,
one suggested two days' pay.

And in that second light, Gionvanni promised an anniversary:
on his death date to descend, God's breath, out over
pale waters, into Purgatory, to deliver—even us, a sign,
for what Jesus can do for the split-hearted;
though who would notice Francis come down, this kiss,
dirt and wounds to any, by then, ruby-crowned,
fully-fleshed head?

On earth, red lines of pain mapped the force
and reel of Francis' blood in open air. He held them,
his hands on his lap, like a couple of dying birds, qualling,
or behind his back, fingers that couldn't grip, gripping fingers.
Leo had to tear the cloth off, away from his hands, side,
would nearly swoon beneath the piercing cries of heaven.

St. Francis Poems

    Francis left the mountain to his friends. Where he was going,
they could not follow, yet, as Jesus told Peter. And finally,
with Leo beside him, he rode back to St. Mary of the Angels.
He gave his hands to his brothers to touch and kiss,
the pain of living, an opened wound, the heart of God,
its slow beat and decline.

    He wanted to die on common dirt, feel cold ground
seep into the dust of his flesh.
He wanted to feel it take him in.

Lyrics based on the *FIORETTI*

I
_____

In this book are contained certain little flowers,
namely, miracles and devout examples of St. Francis
and some of his holy companions.

He was what he lacked, though someone had to be
that too: a divided heart—on his sleeve, God's good
out walking; no difference between him and the birds:
his skin or the rocks, the trees from where he stood.

He had his Judas, John from Capella—the dog
or his tail: strewn ganglia; the foolish man stored
what he had to give. He finally hung himself:
his grin as ballast, a weight no man can afford.

Another, Brother Giles, who wandered his way
up the steps of heaven, his bare feet slapping the clay
and marble of sun-baked hills, his only song:
the life he'd found on the ground—an insect's day.

And one Filippo Longo, who took the world
to his lips like Isaias—walked with a wounded gait;
a Silvester who hurt God through the edges of leaves,
who spoke him wherever he went. They kept their fates

to themselves, except on some days when the sky would wide
open and mouth its icy blue vowel, these wights
whose robes would steam a little in rain—and a fifth,
who left his will to mimic Francis, a light,

St. Francis Poems

so like it that only God could tell them apart;
and Bernard, who explained one scripture with the speech
of another: the woods; or the Brother who, because
the world was too much, kept hiding in trees—past its reach.

There is nothing here but the standing water, a spring
to no one. Even the birds can't hear it sing.

Lyrics based on the FIORETTI

II

Of Brother Bernard, first companion of St. Francis.

A cape into penitential fields—or the moon's
scowl standing in water: both offered nothing but loss;
through two of heaven's years he'd bided the time
that took him, that made the wilderness a cross.

Though once he'd learned he'd never arrive, this saint,
this wound began to draw people: a wealthy man
with the least to give in the whole of Assisi, Bernard,
who'd invited him over for a talk—a stand

of trees in money's rooms; God asking his waif
again to endure the empty walls of this life,
a linen bed, to sit with the alien
he'd become: a fool who taken dirt for a wife . . .

Out of place in any place, St. Francis schemed,
pretended in his silent curl to find sleep.
So Bernard, a manager, watchful in wealth,
did likewise—each beaver soon sawing away in its deep . . .

"My God, my God," was all Francis said that night:
a voice alive inside its own distress,
into the one who wore him; another place
where call was lullaby, where a no was a yes.

St. Francis had to give all that he could not:
the poorest side of Christ, with no home outside
of the boney remains on the forest floor, so he pitched
in the wind, his need—until the morning's tide . . .

St. Francis Poems

As for Bernard, he loathed this world's porcelain face,
asked if he, too, could play a different part.
St. Francis agreed, though this life was, again, too much
for the breadth of his hands, for his reluctant heart.

So they swayed: the flower and the butterfly,
at mass and prayer–until terce broke through the stained
small windows with its light, the market's noise . . .
Bernard felt new again, gave away the reign

of his diversions, those forms: his tapestries
and cloth, his amulets and vacant chairs
to the poor, who would surely not be helped by them,
to prophetic widows who wind our only stair;

his coins to orphans, whose greatest need was a hand
along their backs; to thieves, who'd earned the grace
of smaller cells, whose only horde had been
bad choices; to monasteries—most good at face

and soul; to hospices who could use the seats
to help convey others through the race of time;
to brother pilgrims, who were so to get away
from the whisper of fleeting things . . . It seemed a crime

to Fr. Silvester, a most despondent ear,
nearly deaf from sacrament, from women and men,
no closer to home for all his boxed-in pleas.
His was a rampart in a mortal fen

of swollen feet and gout, a cess of sin,
plus he should have gotten better return for those stones
he'd lugged to St. Damiano, so they could fix
God's church, time itself perhaps! . . . More coins for his home,

a sack to widen his floor! He could say goodbye
to every ripped and lousy chair, his slate
grey table, his single folklore carving, to rooms
one cubit too small since this world began—its bait.

Lyrics based on the FIORETTI

But that night he dreamed: what he owned stacked up in a field;
the birds in song, and Francis giving hands
of cupped water. And so he, too, gave his nothing away,
his small pile: his life as it was, a heavenly van

of mistakes, his worn floor . . . When he became a friar,
he'd speak to Christ as if dispensing a shave.
And Bernard, he became so holy—other, he seemed
a second founder, his opened mouth, his grave.

St. Francis Poems

III

How St. Francis, on account of an uncharitable thought which he had concerning Brother Bernard, commanded the said brother that he should tread three times on his throat and mouth.

Half blinded by the stress and buzz of this world,
his intransigent heart, St. Francis called his home:
Bernard—that those tears might wash his own, called him
into the woods that had dressed him, clothed his moan—

"Come Brother, give light to this blinded man." But Bernard,
so much a part of the different prayer that called
to offer him, couldn't hear the will of God . . .
So Francis deserted the wood, fretting the stalls

he'd wrought, an obsessive past which had led them to this.
He collapsed, a small-minded man in front of the thorns
who'd woven him this wooded crown, at a loss,
repenting for everything but his need to be torn.

And Jesus answered, gave his feet good ground . . .
though soon, again, he was at Bernard to accuse
himself of sin so dyed to the root that he
could never hope to escape its persistent rouse.

For his part, Bernard saw God's nose in front of his face—
a torn man whose tears had planted and grown him from
the weeds that had wreathed his useless wealth—threw himself
at Francis' feet, waited for his life and sum.

And sure enough, grieving over the time he'd lost,
over years he wasted in his courtly shows,
St. Francis raised up God Himself in Bernard:
"I command thee, my friend, with thy docile will in tow

Lyrics based on the FIORETTI

to do what I ask of thee"—and so the son,
who knew the ways of his father all too well:
the truth of his ordinances, responded in turn,
"If thou promise to trade with me, a clap for a bell."

St. Francis, impatient, nodded, because he knew
no other way to be, so flooded with grace,
in the middle of his desires: whirling straw.
So he buried his face into that manger place.

"Now press one foot upon my mummer's mouth,
the other on this hall of lies, my throat;
then tread my guile and over my trumpet's throne
three times, for my brain plays both the rabbit and stoat."

Bernard did as much, but gently enough to shield
a fallen leaf. Then he asked a disciple's boon:
that St. Francis, every time he saw him, that he
should reprove, loudly, each of his defects, his dooms.

St. Francis marveled, for he could see none, nor him—
since he was nearly blind. So he played the fawn
and skirted his only friend, which might have been
a good, for who could have borne such carrying on?

St. Francis Poems

IV

How the angel of God proposed a question to Brother Elias, and because Brother Elias replied to him haughtily, departed, and went along the road to San Giacomo, where Brother Bernard was, and told him this story.

At the call of St. James of Galacia, Francis came
upon a lily, trumpeting its need
along the roadside: a man—torn petals lifted
like patience itself, a hallway to where we bleed,

cathedraled inside our dimness and sin: his cross.
So Francis left his legacy, Bernard;
to offer his disciple this gift, both time
and its end: where to give is hard, and to need is hard . . .

In Spain, a maimed Jesus, still hungry for his heart,
revealed how far St. Francis' feet would tread . . .
It was a weird pilgrimage, this traveling
to hear how far he'd travel, how distant his dead.

So it was in thankful ignorance that he
collected Bernard, returned to his wood, a bole,
a hollowed abyss, his heart without relief.
He crouched inside his hut to pay the troll . . .

Meanwhile at the brothers' door, a lad
banged loudly to test their hinges. Angelic, he packed
each knock with need, the urgency of truth.
And Brother Masseo, the porter, with his sack

of blessings, gave greeting and a lesson: how
to knock one's way into the friar's world—.
He told him Francis was sanctifying the woods.
But the lad said never mind that. He wanted that pearl

Lyrics based on the FIORETTI

of wisdom: the learned Elias. Masseo raised
a brow ... But that mind, so busy with his mound
of leaves, didn't want to be disturbed by a flame
so recently lit—or by any other sound.

So Masseo had to trundle back to the door,
now stuck between a lie and a rude place,
delaying, in circles—to more of that knocking, still
the wrong kind. He sighed at his plight, then pulled the face

of the door again. But this time it was the beam
of youth who instructed, "Go tell your guiding hand," ...
And Francis' voice from the wood: "Go speak to the poor
Brother Elias, hear them—make their demands."

And so the brilliant grudgingly went forth;
but the visitor was, again, the one who would say
this tale: "Take care, for anger belongs to God.
Tell me, is it mete for a man to tighten His ways?"

Still angrily hovering around everything
he knew, Elias slammed shut the only door
out of his world. A step back inside, though, revealed
the question's barb, because this trendy bore

had just decreed against the eating of meat.
So Elias went back to the threshold to—nothing, a shout
from Francis in the wood: "Thy vanity makes
thee a sorry net. You must cast those fishes out!" ...

And at that same hour the youth appeared to Bernard
in a distant wood ... "Whence cometh thou, good teen,
through these quiet bells of morning?" ... Their laughter twined
and carried the friar over a river's between.

"What is thy name?" asked Bernard. "Marvelous,
and so shall we be!" ... And later, seated close to a fire,
Bernard remained in that angel's light-hearted thrall,
happy to serve the proddings of his sires.

St. Francis Poems

V

How the holy Brother Bernard of Assisi was sent by St. Francis to Bologna, and there founded a house.

For the brothers, honors were misdirection, hell's
last smile; to be assaulted with words or stones
was substance of a death to be worked for, proof
of nothing. The world got their ragged backs and bones.

And the changes would come: like Paris strawberries, crepes
in May—the next face of Europe. Take Bernard
against the fascist state, or Marshall's plan,
who was sent to Bologna without a gun or guard.

Adults and children, instruments of ennui,
took turns in yanking his hood . . . To get the full
effect, he sat the piazza, hit with the first stone;
kids rammed him, some calling themselves the Papal bull.

For days he returned, with darkening bruises, but not
to say "the cross" or "how my excesses pain me."
(He slept in a culvert near some scratching dogs,
a frigid silence to keep him company.)

A lawyer, master of fictions, watched his eyes,
which were the same, in the day or under the moon.
Who'd sent this man, he wondered, so punctual?
And what did he hope to accomplish by being gooned?

"Who art thou?" he asked, and Bernard, a man without
a name, drew out the rule. He followed, dumb,
in a lope, as the leader read it, wording their way
to the stones he'd piled. What was this turn that had come?

Lyrics based on the FIORETTI

By the following day Bernard had become the news!
Just by staying there, in an important place,
the people could finally understand—but what,
he wondered? Some wanted to touch him, so he retraced

his steps, enjoined St. Francis to send someone new;
or Bernard might lose more by cake than he'd gained by stones.
And so St. Francis sent the least likely man
to speak the trees, to banish every home.

St. Francis Poems

VI

How St. Francis blessed the holy Brother Bernard
and appointed him his vicar, when the time came
for him to pass away from this life.

Bernard, in mottled sunlight, suffered dark wills
so strong that he had to fall on his face—in the grace
of terror . . . "Brothers, where is my first born son?"
But the prodigal withdrew in that crowded place,

sent someone else . . . "My sons, this isn't the head
of my body," St. Francis said as he groped, then dropped
back on the bed, almost despairing because
he just wanted God, to do the will that had cropped

him. But what if he were wrong again? . . . Then his hands
found two of his heads: Bernard and the burning red
of Elias (Old Testament foil, a needy "instead").
"Whoever blesses thee, my heir, shall be led

by grace to wear the hairshirt of his flaws." . . .
And from his weakness, Bernard became both bell
and lead cow. The friars would learn to line up behind
him, proceed in their back and forth, down through the dells.

Though when his time came to settle into death,
he was interrupted—again: his brother Giles
who offered him the truth of our station, cried out:
"Sursum corda . . . sursum corda"; there are miles

in every inch! And so, though his body wracked,
Bernard got up. He marshalled his grieving crew
to sweep out a leafy cell, a place where Giles
might wash the world to its sunny elbows, lose

Lyrics based on the FIORETTI

himself in the light between the summer leaves . . .
And hoisting himself again, Bernard offered peace:
"Most beloved Brothers, I will not speak many words;
but consider that the religious state must increase

in you as this hour will also come as your life.
I find in my soul, that for a thousand worlds
as good as this, I would not have served a lord
more negligible than ours . . . Myself, I hurl

at your feet, and ask that you give and bless my leave.
Love one another as I have not loved you." . . .
And after these words, and a ramble on some herbs
and the gaits of various birds, he lay on his pew.

His face grew younger, measuring the life
which had meted out his steps—his departing friends
and a young angel marveling on the road . . .
Another unlikely chapter come to an end.

He'd been a ragged leaf, fallen, the ground
of our being—as much as our endless fictions can bare.
Mice gathered for cards on the shadowy forest floor,
in the company of stars. The future is there.

St. Francis Poems

VII

How St. Francis passed the Lent on an island in the Lake of Perugia, where he fasted forty days and forty nights.

In the dew: bear dances, Bruegel laughter, ale froth
and mud, so Francis skirted the stalls, the fair,
chose Lake Perugia, a friend's repose—
where fewer jugglers could rummage through the air

for misplaced choices. He chose instead to fight
the only past that counts: in his heart, on its isle.
With two loaves of bread to knock together, he begged
for more wound to always lead him—beneath the smiles

of temptation, under that palest of moonlight barks,
his four fingers pulling through the watery glass.
Stars folded in the plum sauce as weeds approached:
the world as it had been, for a boy on the grass—

the morning thickets on that island, a cell
in a blind, in a generosity of leaves . . .
He prayed when he could and then when he couldn't, when
the cost of his body paid him with glare or bees.

How much of the shadow of self-promotion hung
on him there, did his brainpan shrivel in the sun?
And did that mirror take on the second tongue?
Did he flail himself on the grass, his Lent now begun?

Eating his sins he chose the harder half
of the loaf, knew that he had to be poured out again,
and again . . . He prayed to stay where his heart revealed
the truth of his lies: the needs in every man.

Lyrics based on the FIORETTI

Crushed, he'd be both God's wheat and chaff, the king
loving too well to leave the thing undone.
(Each seed sheds husk, its fibers—for a tongue:
pale fetus to lithesome green, so moist it stuns.)

And miracles came through the years because
there was room for growth: new folk who began to construct
fine houses there, inhabit them in rows
in the greatest simplicity; and still later to cluck

in a newer village yet, dull burghers and fries,
a slew of energetic young girls, and a famed
new friary which is called The House of the Isle.
And to this very day, the men and dames

of the village put down rushes to walk on, hush,
because they have such reverence and pride
for the spot where Francis made his happiest Lent . . .
You can hear his pennywhistle from God's other side.

St. Francis Poems

VIII

How St. Francis showed to Brother Leo
what are the things in which consists perfect joy.

They felt frozen stiff, like a rumbling truck half full
of icy turnips; St. Francis trudged through his sins
in bare feet, worn cloth, behind Leo—the slow:
like farmers from Perugia, razed in

the wind, both threadbare, their skin to winter skies,
much as they'd always been, the elements—home.
So Francis called out ahead and named him "Blood,"
"Oleander": bitter . . . Leo walked alone,

ahead of his storm: "Oh, Brother," Francis reached,
deploying each syllable as if it might greet
the need: "Great example surely isn't joy."
(Apparently not—thought Leo who felt for his feet.)

" . . . nor in miracles . . . nor in knowing every text
and scripture . . ." (Nor in any string of discursive bells.)
And on he went, like the road, like this winter life:
"Nor tongues of flame . . . nor converting infidels . . ."

For miles he wagged. "No, no, it's not there, my friend.
Nor at table, nor in the quill, the hides of lambs,
nor in the warm and inn side of a wall.
And if we were to get thrown out on our hams,

into a colder night, and were to bear
that without murmuring as dumb oxen do,
and were to say in the caverns of our hearts
that lord surely knew us; and if we stirred the stew

Lyrics based on the FIORETTI

of that keeper's rage: if our hands ached as we knocked,
and if he were to drive us away with kicks
and buffetings; and if we returned, so gaunt
that our bellies seemed a hazel-knot, and ticks,

our friends; and if he were to growl, erupt,
come out with a bulbous club and seize us by
our worthless hoods and spin us over and roll
us, kick us into snow and beat us to sighs,

on our welts until they ripped our habits' seams;
and if we spoke with only the joy of our sores . . .
Ah, Brother, now there would be such peace, complete
as the great height of any hearth, the pour

and toast and beneficent tale. There we would find
answer enough, my friend, to be our calm
and spinning boeuf, our flowered omelettes.
For over all the graces is the balm

of purest ignorance: of conquering self.
There failure is gain. So let's not waste the time,
the snow, whatever we feel; how else shall we grow
in the cold before sun, in these almost equitable climes?"

St. Francis Poems

IX

How St. Francis taught Brother Leo how to answer him, and the brother could not say anything but the contrary of what St. Francis desired.

St. Francis, in the throws of their noisy start,
sat down with Leo into what mattered, no book
to guide—just another stalk that shakes the wind
for what it needs, the two of them, by the look

of it, against that lapdog: our speed for love.
So he instructed his disciple to say
"In truth, my maw, for thy sins and thy ravening guts
thou deserve the hell that would sharpen its knives and flay . . ."

(Li Po's worm was made to dance the wren!)

". . . 'O Brother Francis,' say, 'thou hast surely racked
up so many pretty garden party wrongs,
drama woes, that they overload your pack.

Thou like the greater part of the dog: mankind,
hast merited hell to roast thee in thy turn.'"
But when Brother Leo opened his mouth, only birds
came out: "Our God will work such good as you yearn,

across the doormat of your life, the weave
itself shalt flower with the passing of feet,
and thou shalt have a home on sun-splashed heights." . . .
St. Francis, though, would never hear of retreat;

and so Leo fought with himself, meeked: "I speak
in the name of God, this time I will answer true." . . .
And Francis, again, continued his inward turn:
"O Brother Francis, thou insignificant mule,

Lyrics based on the FIORETTI

too stupid to take even one good step, dost thou think
our God will have mercy on such reticence?
What wilt thou ever do?" And again, Leo,
or someone very much like him, ignored the defense:

"Yea, rather, thou shalt receive great graces from God—
like honey and rain they shalt fall, because he who finds
himself in the dirt shalt own it, and more, and I
cannot say otherwise, for Jesus binds

thy will and my mouth with both of his wounded hands." . . .
And in this humble boxing match, both men
held fast to what they knew—and had to say,
until the world was changed from the lie it had been.

St. Francis Poems

X

How Brother Masseo mockingly said to St. Francis that all the world went after him; and St. Francis replied that this was for the confusion of the world and for the glory of God.

"What is the square root of duck, the meaning of fish?"

Sure, he'd given him place, but the man would fall
out of the woods, behind birds, caught in his sleeves—
twigs besting his cowl. So Masseo asked, "Why the rout,

of common sense, I mean?" And Francis, who played
each hand he'd been dealt, replied: "What wouldst thou say?"
"Thou art not a man who glitters when he walks,
nor were you born beneath a steward's sway;

your stature is straight enough, slight though it be,
but you know neither religion nor the stars;
for what reason does the world run after thee?"
St. Francis, who could see the road, but not far,

rejoiced, caught up in the laughter of the Christ,
who just then stirred some great white clouds with a bite
of breeze, moving the chorus: the limbs of trees.
The poor one dropped to his knees and spoke. "You're more right

than you know. For he could find no viler man." . . .
He knelt there in silence for a time, then stood.
"And for this he's elected me to mud the huts
of the noblest men, to codify the woods;

to give dead limbs and storms to the rich, this flesh
to the strong, to count fleas for the courts, a tongue so tied
since my birth that it takes the world from the wise; that men
may know what they've always known: our Lord's bloody side.

Lyrics based on the FIORETTI

None of this is new." And Masseo understood
that Francis was twin to the forest's feral hogs,
their grunt in the grasses, a part of the mercy that owns
each liar in the world—each hearthside log.

St. Francis Poems

XI

How St. Francis made Brother Masseo turn round and round, and then went on to Siena.

Among the charred and vacant, St. Francis lagged
behind; while an active agent, Brother Found,
worked through the issues that made the future tense,
hoped for some colors beside the present brown.

And when the world seemed to agree: which way
to Florence, Arezzo? Masseo felt confirmed—
though humility stayed the best of him: he asked,
"Which way do we go?" . . . "The way of the bird and the worm."

"But how can we know his only and perfect will?"
So Francis set him to spin—as children do,
though they delight in the unknowing, falls,
and Masseo could not. Still he held to what he knew.

He fretted: perhaps he should be enjoying this game?
But Francis would not let him gather his thoughts.
And so his world continued its spin, as it had
forever it seemed. But why so long? . . . He'd wrought

the kettle he stewed in, but who else *could* he be?
He got no answer as Siena and
his wits, upon command, soon gathered in-
to view . . . How much correction could he stand?

As they walked, Masseo plied his trade with care:
he got the metaphor, the unwinding school,
but why had Francis played the child before
these seculars who often deemed them fools—

Lyrics based on the FIORETTI

that surely wouldn't help the stereotype.
Once in Siena, though, he was saved from his thought . . .
Both were hoisted, as if this choice were the only way,
were bounced like kings to the Bishop's house. (The folks sought

a cure for the town's disputes, its civic dead.)
And the saint, because he had nothing important to give,
could offer them the peace that drove him, bring them
the ache of God and the place where each one lived . . .

Relieved, with a settled flock, the bishop asked
St. Francis to share the flush of wine and the glint
of fellowship, by day and into the night.
Masseo had never expected this, this hint

of a bustling life . . . But since Francis never gave
himself to sleep, he gathered his hungry birds,
and set off before dawn, without taking the Bishop's leave.
Masseo fretted for miles about the words

they never spoke, the kindly prelate's made
and rejected bed . . . But then he cast out that lie:
"Siena hath proven itself an humble road.
And if Francis bids thee throw stones thou ought to abide."

(Masseo was good at throwing stones.) Might he
ask him to do that? He wouldn't . . . And right on cue:
St. Francis' hand on his back. "Those seeds thou now sow
will find good soil. But thy first spread would do

neither you, nor the birds, nor the ground any good. Your reach
was hell's." Then Brother Masseo saw clearly that
this man knew his heart. And he was glad—because
St. Francis had never cast him out on his hat.

St. Francis Poems

XII

How St. Francis imposed on Brother Masseo the office of the door, and of the kitchen, and of the almsgiving: and afterwards, at the prayers of others, released him.

St. Francis Van Gogh, his ear so in the world
beyond that people wondered if he spent
enough time here. He spoke like wind to the trees,
on a track too far from our jump. So the friars bent

in to hear, even as Masseo was offered his life:
"Thy brothers are herons who have the gift of wait
and contemplation. They need our leave to peel;
and since you, a stalwart wagon, have to rate

the gift and rut of compromise: the noise
of the day in your preaching, that you may know both the rhyme
and the silence that has formed us all, perform
the door, the kitchen, and almsgiving for a time.

And when they eat, to give them more room at board,
take thy world and plate and sup at the door on thy haunch—
with the mice so that you might know all little things." . . .
Masseo felt so stunned that the saint would launch

him with a gift of preaching—since he had seen
his brothers glide recollected like giant ships—
that he drew his hood and hurried to his place.
(His father's plan gave each ship a perfect slip.)

But his companions, since they were not removed
from this present world, and did not like the me,
the sting of privilege as they watched him hump
about like a house guest trying to fit—where he

Lyrics based on the FIORETTI

does not belong—lined up before the saint,
their shaven heads neatly bowed. Their least then asked
to share their brother's joy. So Francis, surprised
again by the Spirit, would give his birds new tasks.

Masseo, of course, was good with either road:
"My father's directions are the door I trace—
the poorest hand of Jesus—in my dust."
And St. Francis, seeing God's earth in each pleasant face

and hearing the trees in their shake outside the hut,
allowed the spirit to consume him, lift
him through his words. He preached how only the gifts
of God make us smaller by the day, his sift,

until we disappear. We are God's larks
to Himself. And then as father, Francis raised
the jobs like Christmas candy above their hands,
while Masseo choiced the figs, on a distant bay.

St. Francis Poems

XIII

How St. Francis and Brother Masseo placed some bread
which they had begged on a stone beside a fountain;
and St. Francis greatly praised poverty; and how St. Peter
and St. Paul appeared to him.

Feeling crowded by expectations, their long
and holy faces, St. Francis sent them out
with all that they possessed: their sins; then yoked
himself to Masseo's want, for his last bout

with his father's France. En route, the two of them came
to a sow run of a town, with too many kids
chasing beasts, old women in their final crofts;
another place brimming with good needs and bids

to meet them . . . It was time to beg for his bread.
And because St. Francis was smaller than his size:
ungainly, ruddy, with tangled hair, he drew
the first pried morsels of charity: his prize,

a darkened trencher, while Masseo, tall,
a man who had surely just misplaced his way,
was offered a lighter bread from behind hinged doors.
(He bowed, encouraged by the crisp new day.)

St. Francis set their camp near floating fat
in a stream where they placed their bounty: his true worth
and need, the leprosy that would mold those hands.
"O Masseo, who are we to deserve God's earth?"

The other, though, foreseeing only want,
gaunt brothers, replied: "But prophetic Father, we lack
a cloth, the cutlery, the porriger.
Shall our future selves expire along muddy tracks?"

Lyrics based on the FIORETTI

St. Francis looked for a time at his hands--then raised
them: "So it has always been, my friend: for the poor,
who have borne our name well before we knew their face
and could wash their feet with our praise. Embrace their sores:

these things were keen for their tables because we want.
May lady poverty serve us until we are fed." . . .
And after they'd worked their mouths around the rot
and opened their faces to water, St. Francis led

them toward the great and self-sufficient France . . .
But because what isn't is so far away,
they stopped at a church. There Christ took over the saint,
who flushed and then faded white into his sway:

brown face, now vacant with what paled his lips;
his soul like smoke through a screen as love in-breathed
him—a conflagration for all the baffled folk
he had ever known, their names and faces, the sleeves

of their lives . . . And then coming back to his friend, he croaked
in a distant voice: "Ah! Ah! My brother, yield
thyself to me as the spring does to the rose,
as the rising dust does to the roads, the fields."

Three times he repeated this, and by the last
he lifted a so relaxed Masseo up by
his breath that the man's arms seemed to follow him
in a spin, and gave a pure season to the sky

outside. He drifted in every leaf before
their life . . . Then that wind tossed him the length of a spear . . .
Masseo grogged back into the world—a place
he'd never known, a heaven built by tears.

What they reached for that day they found: the spirit which breathes
the world, gives it comfort and form . . . He embraced his home,
the floor, where he heard the will of Francis: "Let
us find the apostles, St. Paul and Peter in Rome.

St. Francis Poems

Let us ask them for our mercy, poverty:
our lady since her want makes pride reveal
itself, makes it writhe in the light of day. She is
his cross and only consolation—a peal

in our lives. May she guard her children with weakest arms,
give us our elders to walk us through these lands." . . .
Once in that church, St. Francis, Masseo both arched,
prayed up the nave which seemed the folded hands

of the cathedral . . . And since heaven's saints live so close
to littleness, Francis turned that corner and met
God in stone: "The Lord Jesus has sent us to give you your wish
which is his; moreover, his blood would grant you yet

more, that your sons might be her rags and call.
And whosoever shall trace thy lead shall own
the heart that bears him thence—by the cut through stone
which reveals the flesh of Christ here: his reach and his home."

St. Francis tripped over to Masseo, whose eyes
were closed, whose molars ground their way—to what?
He had seen nothing but cold floors, his feet,
the world still beneath them, its pilgrims and its ruts.

So Francis gave him the other half of our tale—
one man on earth, one verging into sky . . .
And then it was time to return, to live in the wood.

St. Francis had forgotten his father's sigh.

Lyrics based on the FIORETTI

XIV

As St. Francis and his brothers were speaking of our divine Lord, he appeared in their midst.

Beneath the moon's icy and vacuous gaze, the waste—
a void of voices gutting each empty day:
God as a lie . . . But then trees rustled; he turned
his ear and the river spoke—his only way.

There was nothing new in any of this: the price
to be paid, the burdens of fellowship. So he called
the men, asked each to speak one word from Christ.
And as soon as one brother would, St. Francis walled

him up inside his room of silence again
and moved to the next, until each leaf had blown
itself through the darkest night. (Each person in place—
he could settle beneath the stars he didn't own.)

Their meekness could've made them a moon in the sky,
or a line of green-necked ducklings swimming at night.
And when the last had dunked—the blessed Christ,
the Aperture appeared, bending all light,

the living substance of their words: the ground
which fashions earth, which gives it a face of bone,
the way and truth who offers—exactly himself,
who creates as others breathe, all that we clone

in his busy hands . . . He was more than their bodies could take;
until Francis woke into what he'd become: "Let's bless
our God, who has willed that the wavering mouths of fools
should reveal his power though all he's not. The rest

St. Francis Poems

is his; and we will march and file our days
in hiddenness, below his silent speech,
until the world recovers the war it has lost
and loses its posing, its articulate reach."

Lyrics based on the FIORETTI

XV

How St. Clare ate with St. Francis and his companion brothers
at St. Mary of the Angels.

Sir Francis, a knob of cauliflower, the node
on a dewy branch, set off to visit St. Clare . . .
But when she needed to rest a disciple's head
on his chest, he felt their kinship begin to tare.

"Our father, this stiffness seems unnatural;
unless you can find it in the parables
or in nature," the brothers said . . . "Very well, since it seems
so to those who wise the fence, so it does to the bull.

But we'll eat here with St. Mary and her troupe."
And so St. Clare with one of her sisters left,
escorted by jongleurs, his boutonnières
who squired them to her Lord's new house—bereft

of place: like a field of absent flowers in rain;
too many dirty feet in an out-of-step
round dance. A call to what—with settings placed
on the ground! (Perhaps a trap set by the adept?)

But then Francis opened . . . and got so lost in God
who speaks us alive, and again in the mystery
of his choosing, who's in a rush to deliver us
to ourselves, to finish the parts that must be free.

And as this new community both found
its light and lost its bearings, men from town,
from Betonia behind the flanks of horse
and home, their forging places, turned from their frowns,

St. Francis Poems

their partial answers to see St. Mary's wood
on fire, felt heat from the road. Fearing the worst,
they geared up and ran to help. But when they got
there, heaving in stabs of pain, they gasped and cursed

the good in front of the crumbling hut—where they found
too many nests on the ground, the plaster patched,
a conspicuous silence . . . So fear in hands, they went in,
saw people in robes much older than rags, singed thatch,

heads bobbing back in a swoon, digesting God,
each caught up in a heavenly measure. (None bore
an apron coated in blood and fat!) . . . And when
St. Francis returned to an oddly tracked up floor,

he spoke about the folds of poverty,
about being her useless child; they'd been fed to hear
the voices that mattered—twigs underfoot, the cold,
the heart of the poor, the nothing that they held dear . . .

And St. Clare, well-escorted again by the simple hands
of the saint, returned to St. Damian's where she
could offer no relief . . . They were sure she'd been called
away to graft some other vine, decreed

from them, as Francis had given Sister Lamb
to Monticelli. But no, she said, she'd been sent
here--until they got it right, though she would perch
forever to go, since given lives must be spent.

Lyrics based on the FIORETTI

XVI

How St. Francis received the counsel of St. Clare,
and of the holy Brother Silvester, that he should preach
for the conversion of many; and how he founded the third order,
and preached to the birds.

As he lead his flapping of herons down the road,
St. Francis repented that he had no gifts
to build on here. So he asked, could he pray or should
he burden the noise and preach? What would be his shrift?

He asked his Brother Masseo to go to Clare,
to Silvestro—who spoke with God as if at lunch.
"This is what God says," offered the monk. "Thou shalt say
that Christ hasn't called him to watch his spirit bunch

like flowers after rain. But that he feel
his death so that others might learn to live. Give him hail
to hear that his Lord will be a spoken word."
Masseo then turned to Clare—and the nodding of veils.

Once back, St. Francis washed Masseo's feet
until he could see their beauty again, then led
him into the bracken, spaced trees, where mottled light
had been most of his sight, had offered the absence that fed

him . . . "Let's leave then," he answered, and they left that spot,
with all the courage of ones much better armed.
He gave no thought to the way, but scurried, so fast
that he did his brother's new humility harm.

The village was called Savurniano. And so
he began to preach, with no concern for what
came out, commanding the swallows to stop until
he had finished. He spoke with such ardor: words that cut

St. Francis Poems

his own heart, until the whole village wanted to drop
what they were doing, leave their hammers, homes . . .
St. Francis, shocked, had to reign their zeal back in:
homes had to settle so that the preachers could roam . . .

Along the side of the road, he touched each trunk
at its station: erudition on the way.
But even these came alive with the singing of friends:
each wanting to be counted, to have its say;

and so he cautioned the brothers: "Wait here, my friends,
a little while. I must go and preach God's song
to my sisters, the birds. The earth is clay, but it
is river too. And they must know the throng

that gathers them in." And he began to preach
to those at his feet about the Ground. But the lost
that perched the boughs could not accept their place,
and so flew up and down off branches, which tossed

behind—now silent and earnest in the round:
(like a button in its only hole), so that when
he had finished spelling out duty and degree,
they would not leave the confines of their pen

until he blessed them. And as Masseo would long
after tell the story, St. Francis went deep and out
among them, touching birds with the turns of his cloak.
He called them by made-up names, foreseeing each bout:

erupting wing or beak. The docile earned praise,
and none of them moved until he'd rejoiced in the slant
or tilt of each head. And as St. Francis spoke
their lives to them, they opened their beaks—not to rant

at this hungry world. But instead they stretched their necks,
their wings and bowed a mortal carpet, their heads
to the earth, to show him that his gift of words
had given them mission to go and die in his stead.

Lyrics based on the FIORETTI

The saint then made the sign of God, gave them leave
to depart to their new homes, to live their square feet
of life. And thereupon those birds whirled up
a sky, a chorus of air—and in precise fleets

divided themselves into four. They flew both east
and west, to the south and north, in love with the cross,
renewing St. Francis and his brothers, who would
possess no flight of their own—except in loss.

St. Francis Poems

XVII

How a little boy-brother, whilst St. Francis was praying at night, saw Christ and the Virgin Mother and many other saints talking to him.

Awake at night, with no family bed or tales,
no mother's hands or voice to quiet trees,
the slashing rain as he lay, small soul, in a world
of truckle beds, under sweat and cracking knees—

the snores; as near as he could to Francis, who would,
long after prayer, in the buzz of flies, slip away.
The boy needed to know where he went—to what ritual,
adventure, so he bound their cords, a tight sway

to signal the time, but loose enough to give . . .
St. Francis rose to untie the predictable schemes
of this world and walked out into the mouth of the night,
into a cell where he traded sleep for tight seams

of light . . . The boy startled to find the cord, put his face
behind him and walked the path into the dark wood.
He heard much speaking—and so forgot his way . . .
And then he saw them all through the leaves, his first good:

a glimpse of heaven among the chirps, a bright man
not much bigger than he: St. Francis—and the Son!
The green world bent into him, its way and feed;
and humility: his mother, who looked like a nun;

seated on a rock . . . the face of the Baptist, aglow!
And the Evangelist, who was shorter than all
except Francis, with wings to rival the multitude:
a crowd of angels—some high above in a brawl

Lyrics based on the FIORETTI

of feathers, some flanking in the nave of limbs,
around the one. But because each fuss was so close
to heaven in motion and spiel, the lad fell to the earth
like a nut . . . St. Francis, stumbling through a dark dose

of this world, tripped over the brother who, sunk among
its roots, lay sequestered; the saint then lifted him up
as best he could. And in the morn, having learned
how central the night had become, he sought to dim

it through obedience. The lad was not
to tell a soul as long as Francis should serve
on the altar of time. And the boy grew in vigor, peace:
like the founder, a background man, his tenuous nerves

forgotten, happy with the smallest place . . .
And after the death of the poorest one, his tale
was added to those which had so mastered him,
so that other inmates could learn the pace of the snail.

St. Francis Poems

XVIII

Of the marvelous chapter which St. Francis held
at St. Mary of the Angels, at which were present
more than five thousand Brothers.

In a valley of daffodils, each with no place
or reason to lay his head (or brown-eyed susan's
a-flutter: schoolgirls in a lively breeze).
Who'd have thought that life had undone so many—again?

St. Dominic-of-his-way, though, on his cool
and studied course from Borgogna to the see
in Roma had to account the thousands himself.
And a Perugian Cardinal, too, came to free

himself in this comedy of charity,
each brother filling the cup for his own: "These knights
are the truer templars of the crucified.
This is the crusade we sought, Christ's visible plight

and song." The brothers' tents were hung upon
the willows, in mats of rush, under trees and the moon;
positioned stones made for provinces, though none
abided, each friar on God's own. So they soon

began to name themselves, "The chapter of mats,"
or "of the trellises," or "of this ravine."
Their bed was the ground from which they sprang, and they found
the warmth they sought in night talk, in the straw they'd gleaned;

for pillows they had the mossy stones, or their arms
or logs of wood—and memories of home . . .
Their hiddenness drew the busy eyes of those
who counted—themselves: on draped horses in the gloam,

Lyrics based on the FIORETTI

the flourish of ownership; and the glances, too,
of parish priests, graced abbots, they all came to see
this lowest rung of heaven—Francis, the end,
a fool who took in each stiff: the "us" and the "me."

"My sons, so great is the providence of God
that the fall leaves fizz yellow, cry out his name.
This world is the rapture of his voice. But its call
must not stay us. We have our work: to tame

ourselves. So we can't be bound by the demands
it makes. Laughter of lilies, I command you to stand
and have no care for food, or for where you'll die
since he lifts you up like water into his hands . . ."

St. Dominic, though, who'd been lessoned by his dreams
and had seen the needy orphaned girls of Spain,
knew that prudence demanded earnest husbandry—
or the men would certainly all end up like Cain . . .

But flowers get by with the sun, and the local folk
from Perugia, Spoleto, Foligno, with mules
and carts came, each laden with their lives' red wine,
the bunch in grapes. In mindless cheer new rules

chased brothers around, each trying to out-serve
the rest. Great knights and gentlemen who counted—
(again) themselves, who'd come to be amused,
now snapped green beans . . . St. Dominic dismounted.

"No Brother in my order shall own any land." . . .
And Francis, with an ear for the dove, followed suit:
he forbade leather bands, sharp-pointed chains—more than
five hundred of the latter, a cache of loot

which included circlets for the arms and loins.
(He left them there, in the field, that the crickets and rain
might eat them, teach them to rust in forgiving soil.)
Concluding, St. Francis left his own with a stain:

St. Francis Poems

that each moment might be filled with blood, and with
the cage of heaven shaking the naked trees.
He dismissed them to the halls of the woods, each place
enlivened with a chorus of bending knees.

Lyrics based on the FIORETTI

XIX

How the vineyard of the priest at Rieti, in whose house St. Francis
rested, was despoiled of its grapes, and afterwards miraculously
yielded more wine than heretofore: and how God revealed
to St. Francis that he should have paradise for his portion.

His eyes were dim—the way he'd always been,
out nosing among dead leaves: too slow to stand,
too quick to sit down. So if his Lord had need
of this last and hesitant dance, he could take his hand,

as his brothers had done these days. Besides, they all
were in tow here—as his dirty half-formed band
set off on another cardinal song. They stopped
at Clare's, his eyes, like wilted blooms in his hands.

He saw men like trees, trees like the fall of man,
and smelled the metal in his insistent blood
as he tried to hide the pain he felt when touched.
Misunderstanding, St. Clare gave him the mud

of a hut where he might rest from company.
Without his eyes, he had to endure rats' feet
as they scratched a horde of innuendo along
the walls, at his robe. How could he lie down, or eat?

He could get no rest, either during the day or at night;
a victim of prayer, his friends left him alone.
It was all he could do to keep from crying out.
This was the other side of Palm Sunday's stones—

for his sins, and for those tendencies he'd passed
to the brothers. (People thought too much of this cur.)
He knew the state of the house in which he lived:
its stink and bad turns, the fouled cockroached corners.

St. Francis Poems

This was the purge no man escapes—the truth
of his life. He lead with his hands and felt along
those internal walls, his breathing the only sound,
except for no prayer which gave the night to his wrong . . .

"Rejoice, Sir Francis," said Christ. "I'll give you a chair
large enough to embarrass, a gilded catacomb.
An increase of joy brings sorrow. How could it be
another way—until all the lambs are home?"

Relieved, St. Francis held both of Clare's small hands
in his own, then bowing a little to the right,
he winked at her and with his attending monk,
took his leave to finish what was left of his sight . . .

As they approached Rieti—more threats that he
couldn't see: many came to gawk, but all to see.
So the brothers lead him to a church two miles
from town . . . It didn't work. Folks circled, their pleas

alive with zeal, or something very like that.
In haste, they trampled the vines—and its owner died,
like each person does when he consents to love:
another faulty vision crucified.

But Francis had a heart much larger than
his own: "Good hands of Christ, how many sacks
of wine have the cuttings left you in your best
year under heaven and the merciful backs

of your servants?" "Twelve." "Please allow this feast for a few
of these days, and let who will come home, for the heart
of God and for me, his useless little clown,
and eight more measures shall you find, as seas part."

And so St. Francis, pressed about by souls,
the huge and singular presence of each child
and woman, their needs, could offer just the lord
who owned him, pouring himself because his guile

Lyrics based on the FIORETTI

was gone. And many went away cured or whole,
bent on abandoning the world that day;
the vineyard trampled, scarcely one cluster upon
the next, not one of them fit . . . So the brothers delayed

in their going, re-set the vines and gathered the grapes . . .
And when the cleric trampled his months, that gain
in his mind, as he coaxed his tiny yield—of course,
he got his measures—that year and those after . . . stained!

Who can believe these stories? Besides the folk
who read them, that is? Nobody—at least at first.
Then you realize you need the grapes, the wine.
How else would the world be drawn into His thirst?

St. Francis Poems

XX

Of a wondrously beautiful vision seen by a young brother.

Did his scratchy habit expose his divided heart,
the smelly him it carried: an old, wet barn?
Its angry sleeves invented lice—felt like roots
in dark and occupied waters. The hood was darned,

ungracefully knit; it whispered charade. And the coarse
weave offered no give: it bagged the saint that he
would never become . . . He'd known the greasy till,
but that had spat him out—unerringly.

Forever between, he wearied of this leash:
his director's order to prostrate before the bread
each hour, his feet the only sound he could hear.
Yes the quit would surely take him—to where he'd been fed.

His last time . . . interrupted by a noise,
by the carousing of other-worldly louts:
saints clad in a fiery glaze of transfigured cloth,
embroidered calls, by gold and silver shouts,

by cyan and daffodil, with such peace, such rough
and robust glory—plush buttons and a bloom
of chestnut hoods . . . The two most nobly attired,
almost hidden in the midst of the lavish loom

and pomp, in a torrent of fine stitchery,
seemed taken aback by the rowdy march, its pace
and beauty, trying to time their steps as they sang
in the song . . . Our brother watched well beyond the brace

of those two going. And then, at the end he caught
a third, so adorned for his glorious final course

Lyrics based on the FIORETTI

in the widest hat, that the man appeared as though
he were a new-made knight being led to horse

and honor and a final throne, with friends . . .
Then the brilliance passed with the last sounds of feet
as they slapped the slates . . . The brother chased his heart . . .
"We are all of us friars who have found our meat

in heaven. We have come down to show the least
of the brothers that dilation." . . . "Who were the two,
small in such gold?" . . . "The meek who have given all:
Sts. Francis and Anthony . . . And the last is a fool

who lately died, whom I name Brother Persevere,
because his road ran, like everyone's, right up
until the end. But now that's over, its truth
begun. See how he drinks, at last, from the cup

as it really is. Our rough habits were our poor
and only answer, our insufficient song.
So don't let the sackcloth of your life disturb
your goal." . . . These words heard, our youth returned to the wrongs

he knew: to his life like a tent with too few poles.
And knowing how much he was cherished, the brother fought
the face of ease and lived in the roughness of cloth:
the place that gave him the only comfort he sought.

St. Francis Poems

XXI

Of the miracle which St. Francis performed
when he converted the wolf of Gubbio.

In a surer Christian time, the same old past
chose to swing its muzzle toward Gubbio: in a spate
of sullen teens, suspicious mates. Folks ate
their grief because death now scratched at the hasps of its gates.

In their angst they beat sticks and shouted when it came close
because they were too afraid to send it away.
(Townsmen carried pikes outside the walls—
as far as they dared, victims of their own delay.)

So Francis, who felt the tumid constriction—as streets
couldn't breath beneath the contempt that owned them, the sealed
up lives—would go to the wounded beast, though hands
tried to hold him back . . . First he blessed the opened fields

as he made his way almost alone toward
their guilt, their reasons to quit. The crowd behind,
the wolf as it circled might've claimed their worlds,
but Francis, who had no home on earth to bind

him, cut through the pomp with two slices of the truth:
the cross. Then he bad the wolf buckle, come to its end . . .
Ordered, it did. But because our faults can grow
in the wake they make, the saint sought some fruit, amends.

If the beast would carefully walk in his step, neither men
nor dogs would make it run. "And I promise you pelf,
both food and a hearth-place shall be given you,
for well I know how hunger can turn—on itself.

Lyrics based on the FIORETTI

And let the burden of your past alone."
The wolf then dropped his eyes. "I would have thy hand,
Brother wolf, that thou wilt stay in this vow, without
which I cannot trust thee to thy nature. The land

will not suffer thee." Then Francis, because he knew
mankind, sought to broaden the moment, to make it event:
"Brother, in the name of Jesus, who taught
us, let's go, you and I, and confirm this time we've spent."

And the wolf, disturbingly large for a sheep, walked close
to Francis to show that it understood, was changed.
And the window talkers, all the children, the reaped
and the sown filled the piazza to see the deranged

made straight: "Goliath," but St. Francis turned—
their sin had pushed God, who should be first into
demanding that their needs be better known.
"And much worse than fangs or death are the flames that are due

to those who wait. Do penance for you sins."
The sermon ended, St. Francis sought refuge for
sir wolf by giving himself as surety;
and his friend gave paw—a moment later than lore

would have liked, yes, but it promised to stay and work
to keep its place. "Brother wolf, I give thanks that you
now pledge our only faith inside the gates
of this place and heaven." . . . And so poverty, her crew,

again changed everything into herself.
As for the wolf, he lived on the fat of the skim,
without harm for two years—and because he was so large,
the people gave way to Francis and to him . . .

Though perhaps they'd just civilized their sin, because
after death, the people did not gather to lay
a fitting stone for either—or for them,
though there is a small wolf selling that square today.

XXII

How St. Francis tamed the wild turtledoves.

A turtledove rattled life against the cage.
The boy, though, was elsewhere: each bird a ticket into
the middle of next week ... Then he met the earth,
brief soul whose dirty feet slapped out the true

language of God: every broken word we say.
And since the two shared the answers that they lacked,
the saint asked that the birds be given back to the wood,
to the sacraments—our lives in gunny sack.

And what would this prophet do with his chosen birds?
Not what the youth expected: he set the brood
on the ground and walked away into the grove.
Coming out with branches, he took to weaving them food:

nests for their sorrows! But how did the man know which
were female? ... He took all of time in hand, and spent
himself. The lad sat and watched him work until
other brothers came ... They stayed and prayed, one lent

him a blanket ... The boy slept next to the cooing birds
and brothers—they seemed the same, and none of these goofs
would depart until matins were said, the sun raised up.
What kind of folk were these? What kind of proof?

The next day every single bird laid an egg;
Perhaps all were girls! ... Miraculous—they hatched.
Then someone gave him bread as he watched the scene,
the hatchling brood soon hopping under patch.

Lyrics based on the FIORETTI

"Small son," that voice and man surprised him, sun
behind the haloed head. "Hast thou learned to bend
and coo in the city of Jesus Christ, our king?"
What could he do, he grabbed the twigs that would send

him far away, to places he couldn't know.
An outsider in an order of them, he found
all he would ever need in swales and mud,
in faces that mirrored his sin—in his passable clown.

XXIII

How St. Francis freed a Brother who was in sin.

A living cloak—each wing to knobby wing,
a bent face here, then there, as it turned, time spent
in creating uneven breezes: a massing swarm
of blackened angst, venal, intransigent.

But none of the devils could loosen a hinge, a seal
because the brothers had given their heartfelt flaws
to the orchestrated discord that was their place.
But having nothing else to do, the raw

wrongs persevered in looking for the kinks
that come, their will that was one day surely done:
a friar found grounds against another, a play
he could believe; and this so stoked up a run

in the brother's mind, that a devil sat on his neck,
a bad half-perch he flapped very hard to keep,
his tattered wings, on worried tendons, knuckles.
He kept in that ear close with the sorry creep

of the world—all for a reward, then another; but
St. Francis, whose vision was not his own, sent the hook
to the fish: a different brother, to call the man
over, commanded him to open the book

of his life: the pages—he couldn't turn. The monk
disclosed the rancor he'd nursed like a bloated calf,
the bile that fed him. And as the man humbly chewed
what was left of the rest of his life, he became the chaff

of the kingdom that comes . . . The boney devil left,
fouling the air, while the not-so-young brother returned
to his youth, to the others, and knew again the death
he needed to feel, the grave that he had spurned.

XXIV

How St. Francis converted the soldan of Babylon to the faith.

St. Francis sought to disrupt the scimitar's arc,
its fertile crescent, where Saracens owned each pass,
were blind enough to kill anyone except
the righteous—. Yet it pleased Jesus that these crass

beggars, no threat to anyone but themselves,
be captured, beaten for their silences
and led before the next soldan . . . St. Francis spoke
the delicate birds of the spirit, said what it says

in hands, baked bean brown and lean: the shape
and show of our lives. And so the pressing lie
that was the soldan, shaken to its knees,
began to feed the restless place that cries

for mercy . . . This ragged minstrel saw the world
as it truly was and stood against its take,
because falsehood can bear no real weight; he chose to bow
his neck to each lie, to the blade that would unmake

itself . . . But the soldan was not taken in,
asked Francis to re-invent his tent with words . . .
He was happy to give the saint and his friends free leave
to preach his truth wheresoever they wanted. He stirred

at the prospect because God's name would be greatly served
this day . . . But at last St. Francis, finding no
more fruit, as people, warned, began to skirt
his lady: her victims, always the first to go.

Lyrics based on the FIORETTI

The holy Muslim called for his friend . . . "Sir Francis,
I would willingly become a song for the faith
of Christ, but we are not alone; for those
who own the truth here would kill both lamb and leaf,

and all thy companions for its humble sake;
and I know by thy speech that thou must live to do
much good; and I also have lesser work. So teach
me how I may be saved from them." . . . The few

and little answered: "My lord, I must go to the land
which owns me; but after my death, as it will please
our God, I will send two bumblers, from whom thou shalt
receive the living water, a home-land breeze:

the Holy Spirit, as has been revealed to me
by our soldan, Jesus Christ. And do thou keep free
from the stroke of fictions which offer a lifeless world.
And then St. Francis, the small, dropped to his knees,

departed. And the soldan, years later, who still
lived in the promise, had watches placed above
the passes, commanding that if a ghost or two
brother moles should approach that they should be brought, in love,

to him . . . And so St. Francis, appeared to two
of the most inconsequential brothers, told
them to go to the soldan. They dropped their brooms and went,
without food or water or fare. They slept in the cold.

And when the caliph saw them he knew the end
of his purse had come; his life had found a late
reprieve, by the merits and prayers of God's smallest grief:
one seed—and the squeeze of the world just has to wait.

XXV

How St. Francis miraculously healed the leper.

He sat amid the charred timbers of his life,
his sin, the leprous ones: so violent,
a patient, not, enraged, that people shrank
from his reptilian grasp. He tore at them, bent

his strength to blaspheme the mildness that mocked him, what was
too motherly to matter, even driving off
the older brothers who couldn't endure this last
inversion . . . Let him enjoin the chorus of scoffs

along the side of the road--but first they went
to Francis, who never turned a need away . . .
No one recognized his cup until he stood
before the old wound: "God give thee his peace, my way

and warning." And then the leper: "What peace have I
from God? I have become a rottenness,
a stink!" And Francis-smell: "My son, have peace;
these ills of the body are your glory. Confess

your sins so that you can see what we seldom do:
the unraveling of all we deserve." The man
replied: "And how can I bear with patience when
I have no room to breathe? I am choked by your band

of brothers as well as by my disease. Why have
you sent them to grieve and wheedle me? They scam
me with their words, will never leave me in
a peace which is no reward?" . . . "Because I am

Lyrics based on the FIORETTI

the least, I will serve thee with unlettered hands.
Since thou hast no stomach for competence, be content
as they find me on their way." . . . "I desire, dust king,
that thou shouldst wash me, because my smell was lent

me by your holy brothers, and I cannot
bear what has become of me." So Francis found
the leaves from sweet smelling herbs; and carefully
disowning his king of his clothes, he began to sound

this Calvary's wounds with his own, while a brother poured
the sheen of water's wing. And by the one
and only miracle, because of the hands
he used, wherever St. Francis touched the son

the wounds departed; and as the flesh found the speed
to knit, so the soul also began to heal
until the man, having been cleaned, commenced
to weep in the first air. His compunction pealed

and drove him to his recovered knees. Now made
anew, he pushed the gall away, said in tears:
"Woe to me, worthy of hell for my flailings, words
and spittings with which I have tried the brothers. I fear

I'm not worthy to loose their sandals. Please let me pay
for my impatient curses against the Good!"
And for fifteen days he circled the camp, moaning
above his sins (while Francis, because he stood

opposed to the self he knew, walked off). Then as
it pleased God, after caterwauling for their spare
prayers, the leper was taken from his sins . . .
On his way to heaven, seated in brightening air,

he came to Francis, who, in a wood, heard it blessed.
The new tramp smiled: "Dost thou know me, little day?"
St. Francis did not. "I am the leper whom Christ
healed through your wounds of love. I go to play

St. Francis Poems

    my life again. Know that there will never be
a day while this world lasts in which the blessed
angels and all the backwater saints will not
thank God for the little flowers which thou and the rest

of your order will bring forth on the greening earth;
and therefore know the comfort you've given. And may
his blessings reach you like points of morning mist . . ."

And saying these words, he jigged off in heaven's way.

Other versions from the *FIORETTI*

VI

Francis blessed the holy Brother Bernard.

It was cold and it snowed
the day Francis died.
The door rattled on its hinges.

Bernard felt the weight of all
he had not done
as he sat on the floor, cornered,
leaning his forehead again and again
into whitewash—his sepulcher:
feeling the dead-wood in his soul,
empty—in the quiet,
in the by now
bird-chirping hours.

It would be another day—
unlike the previous:
the whole world, oblivious
to its own tears.

Francis alone soon would be gone.

There would be other days
Bernard wouldn't want.

And so when the poor one
called for his first born, Bernard
shook like a tired baby:
vicar of the pallet,
first of many wayward children.

XXIII

Francis helps a brother who is in sin.

Francis walked in silence,
one step ahead of another
wronged brother. The sun was setting
and the bark on the trees turned orange.

The two of them sat down on a hill,
first Francis, then the brother.
They watched the moon rise,
shed its column of light
on the water.

Walking back,
Francis, alone with their lives, stopped,
picked up a dead branch.
"Did you know," he asked,
"that the forest has bones?"

He broke the branch over his knee.
The sound echoed through the trees.

"Make a wish—," he said,
"one that's not your own."

Notes

From *The Three Companions of St. Francis*

I His birth, vanity, frivolity and prodigality

FRANCIS COMES ACROSS AS a psychologically healthy fellow, and so I felt the need to jump the original text a bit and have him behave robustly right away: he plays instruments on stumps, sings too loudly before the source has him doing so.

St. Francis surely knew about the troubadours, those wandering Provençal minstrels, who in their beginnings sang and praised our Lady. I imagine him making them his own.

The poem then snaps back to text time, reveals that his father wants him in the family business and so names him after France--in the face of the boy's mother who wanted him named John: Giovanni. I see her concern here as religious: "In the beginning was the word."

II How he was imprisoned in Perugia

Bernart de Ventadorn showed up in some side reading. He seems the only recorded person of that time who actually moved up in class: from baker to minstrel. That fit ambitious Francis, so I brought his story in. That is also why I have Francis singing in bad lange d'oc—though I don't know that there is any historical evidence he knew the language.

One of the real fun parts of writing this poem was that I had to make two outrageous original statements sound plausible: "Rest assured, I will be worshipped throughout the whole world," and "I shall become a great prince."

Notes

And lastly, I know the word "junket" might seem an off note to some, since it's Chinese, but I felt that the sound value trumped the more distant cultural concern.

III How the Lord visited Francis' heart

Francis' concern about a spouse is not mentioned in the original text, but since he was spending so much of his time hanging with his buds, I figured the subject of women had to come up, repeatedly—thus the "crimson stomacher."

VI How he escaped from the persecution

This was fun to write because I wanted to salvage dear old dad, who's always gotten the short end of the history stick. Since I'm a father myself, I tried to see his point of view. Pietro is just speaking common sense to his son. "You know you're going to need food out there," that kind of thing; and Francis is so private and dark about what and who he knows. He would naturally seem weak, willowy to the father.

And dad had to be crushed by the ending of the story. He hadn't wished harm to his son—only prosperity, happiness, the good life as he knew it. So what does he get for his troubles: rejection, humiliation.

Eight centuries of dirt.

Cheer up, dads. Things could be worse.

VII The hard work and fatigue involved in restoring the church

Little Francis, who was barely five foot tall, had to lug heavy begged stones to restore San Damiano. All while his father, as well as his half-brother, continued to harangue him for his childish idealism. Who spends his time all alone, rebuilding forgotten ruins? How was this going to help him get on in the world?

At end, I imagine the beggar Francis coming upon a crowd of his old friends, who here are busy gambling, something not specifically noted in the text.

His weakness was his greatest earthly ally—as ours must be.

Notes

Stigmata Poems from the *FIORETTI*

The first consideration of the holy stigmata
(The mountain is offered)

Orlando de Chuisi was a burdened rich person who sought Francis' help. I include present world imagery in these poems because the issues are always the same.

    The soldier's and the friar's roles are switched in the procession to the given mountain (Orlando's thank you note to Francis). That type of role reversal always seems called for in some way, I think, in orthodox circles since clergymen have historically been so often drawn to clericalism.

The second consideration of the holy stigmata
(Preparation)

Francis's humanity is being emphasized here: a nostalgia he must have at times felt—for earlier, simpler days. (My only experience of this was with observing the "servant-of-God" Catherine Doherty, who surely felt some of that.)

    These medieval stories often veer and take by-ways. Here we hear a story about a young friar, years later, who is being harassed by the same demon that abused St. Francis. Francis, now long dead, saves the falling man because the friar was as simple as the brothers who would find him, singing the bottom of the gorge.

The third consideration of the holy stigmata
(Gifts)

The great miracle begins as Christ appears as a six-winged seraph, comes to meet a levitating St. Francis. The physicality of the stigmata event is emphasized as a milkmaid and muleteers see the bright light miles away—before the rising of the sun.

    Christ then tells Francis that the saint will be allowed to go down into purgatory each year to deliver his followers. May we qualify.

Notes

Lyrics based on the *Fioretti*

I In this book are contained certain little flowers

Francis' twelve is the gist of things here. The last couplet in the collection emphasizes that "we walk by faith and not by sight."

II Of Brother Bernard, first companion of St. Francis

The first images are attempts to capture the feelings of loneliness and destitution Francis must've felt at the beginning. He'd been stripped, was left bereft, and now here he is, asked to bunk with money (Bernard) for the night.

During that stay Bernard catches Francis secretly praying all night and wants in. So the saint takes him to mass and the bible in the morning. God says open the gates, and Bernard joins, gives all his stuff away personally. At this point the narrative takes one of those medieval turns and leads us to a dissatisfied priest, a Father Silvestro, who wants some of Bernard's old cache. He gets his sack of coins, but also the requisite dream.

The priest runs to apologize in the morning, joins Francis as well and later becomes renowned for holiness. That sanctity is the link back to Bernard, who, one of the twelve, also becomes a saintly follower of lady poverty.

IV How the angel of God proposed a question

This chapter begins with Saint Francis pilgrimaging to Spain. He and his small troop find a sick man along the side of the road, and so Francis leaves Bernard to tend to the fellow until they return. The pilgrimage itself seems odd because once St. Francis gets there, God tells him how far his order will reach. Why does God bring him so far just to hear that? Maybe to give Francis a sense of the ardor that the expansion will demand from his disciples.

Anyway, Saint Francis collects Bernard on the way home and goes to his wood; all seems pretty normal if you don't count the angel who's knocking at the friary, in search of the proud Elias. An exchange ensues—which, surprisingly, does not flatter the learned.

Notes

VI How St. Francis blessed the holy Brother Bernard

The Old Testament is worked here with the two sons and the blind patriarch who wishes to pass along his favor. Bernard knows better: he is no Francis. He is no anything—and that of course makes him precisely the man for the job.

The source material then jumps to Bernard's death. He is interrupted by an enthused Brother Giles, and Bernard has to forget his own demise and open to the man, orders that a special cell be built.

Only then does he get back to his last words, which are suitably nondescript, a receipt for another world—both here and there.

VII How St. Francis passed the Lent on an island

St. Francis and Lent. The poem is pretty straight-forward until we begin to move "through the years," nearer the end of the poem. A lot of us miss the central penitential aspect of Francis's life, choose to emphasize the childlikeness. But maybe only part of him would mind that, as we all need to know love first, and deeply, before we can lay our lives down for the Lord God who has suffered and died for us—thus the half-ironic pennywhistle fiction.

IX How St. Francis taught Brother Leo how to answer him

Li Po, an eighth century Chinese poet, drowned as he looked over the side of his boat at his own reflection (or the moon). He was undoubtedly in his cups. The humor of the current scenario involving St. Francis and Leo called on its own for his inclusion.

XII How St. Francis imposed on Masseo the office of the door

The Van Gogh reference is for humor's sake. Had Francis been missing an ear, it would've surely been because it was in the other world. His wishes and commands must've often seemed like communiqués from Mars. (Catherine Doherty again.)

Here he seems to arbitrarily load work onto Masseo's shoulders. But I shift gears and decide to have that brother here take Francis' passing words as ones pregnant with possibility. He is happy to do all the work. Kind of like my kids at home.

Notes

The other brothers, more contemplative, are horrified by the unequal division of labor, so Francis, moved again by the Holy Spirit, redistributes the Christmas gifts—Masseo oblivious to it all as he enjoys his new and coming call.

XIV As St. Francis and his brothers were speaking, our Lord appeared

Here we start with the late temptations of both St. Therese and Mother Teresa: God as a lie. As the poem worked out, that proved to be a helpful start because in the chapter Francis asks for one truth from each brother, then insists on silence. The sequence of events could reveal a frustration with some degree of fraternal pious bullroar.

XVII How a little boy brother saw Christ

A boy lay brother follows St. Francis into the wood at night and is so overwhelmed by the physical action of heaven, "a brawl of feathers," that he falls down as one dead.

XVIII Of the marvelous chapter held at St. Mary of the Angels

St. Dominic's background, where the fate of orphaned school-girls hung in the balance, had taught him the value of a studied prudence. St. Francis's oblivious extravagance—and the countryside which seems entirely taken in by this reckless "goodness"—worries him. The Spaniard learns, as we all must, that there are many ways to skin the nearest cat.

XIX How the vineyard was despoiled

St. Francis, in this late visit to St. Clare's, is suffering from blindness (possibly a symptom of leprosy). He feels drained and is need of consolation, but Clare misreads the situation and gives him a hermit's hut. There nature, his good sister, betrays him in the form of too many rats. He can neither sleep, nor eat, nor pray.

Jesus appears to console him.

Relieved, St. Francis blesses St. Clare and makes his guided way to Reiti, where people pile up to see him at a priest's house. The man's vineyard gets trampled, no end in sight. So Francis promises recompense if the cleric suffers the time; and that prophecy, of course, comes true, as all good stories do—because God knows we need them to.

XX Of a wondrously beautiful vision seen by a young brother

A young friar is harassed by the weight of his habit. He is saved by a heavenly procession. Here again, heaven takes on a physicality which surpasses our earthly experiences. It does so because it is somehow more real than we and this place are.

CPSIA information can be obtained
at www.ICGtesting.com
Printed in the USA
LVHW011803281122
734203LV00014B/1039